It Is Well with My Soul

The True Story of the Writing of the Beloved Hymn

It Is Well with My Soul

The Spirit of Christmas through
ONE FAMILY'S UNFORGETTABLE JOURNEY

As Narrated by **Hugh Bonneville**, with paintings by **Robert Hunt**

Written for the Mormon Tabernacle Choir

by **David T. Warner**

SHADOW
MOUNTAIN

MORMON
TABERNACLE
CHOIR

Mormon Tabernacle Choir is an ambassador for The Church of Jesus Christ of Latter-day Saints.

Art direction by Richard Erickson
Design by Sheryl Dickert Smith

Visit us at ShadowMountain.com

Library of Congress Cataloging-in-Publication Data

Names: Bonneville, Hugh. | Hunt, Robert, 1952–illustrator.
Title: It is well with my soul : the true story of the writing of the beloved hymn / narrated by Hugh Bonneville; paintings by Robert Hunt.
Description: Salt Lake City, Utah : Shadow Mountain, [2018]
Identifiers: LCCN 2018019250 | ISBN 9781629724898 (hardbound : alk. paper)
Subjects: LCSH: Spafford, Horatio Gates, 1828–1888. It is well with my soul. | Hymns, English—United States—19th century—History and criticism.
Classification: LCC BV313 .W37 2018 | DDC 264/.23—dc23
LC record available at https://lccn.loc.gov/2018019250

Printed in China
RR Donnelley, Shenzhen, China

10   9   8   7   6   5   4   3   2   1

THIS IS A TRUE STORY

about a family at Christmastime—
a mother and father who, in the night of their deepest despair,
discovered the healing light of hope.

As it was in Bethlehem, when darkness gathers, the Savior's light shines.
And when His light is reflected in sacred verse and song,
the peace of Christmas, the real Spirit of the Season,
lifts and comforts and blesses us all.

In mid-November 1873, an ocean liner, the *Ville du Havre*, set sail from New York with 313 passengers on board. One can imagine their festive Atlantic crossing with ribbons of red, swags of evergreen, and Christmas carols wafting through a dining room sparkling with candlelight. In a few days they would make landfall in Europe, just weeks before Christmas in Paris.

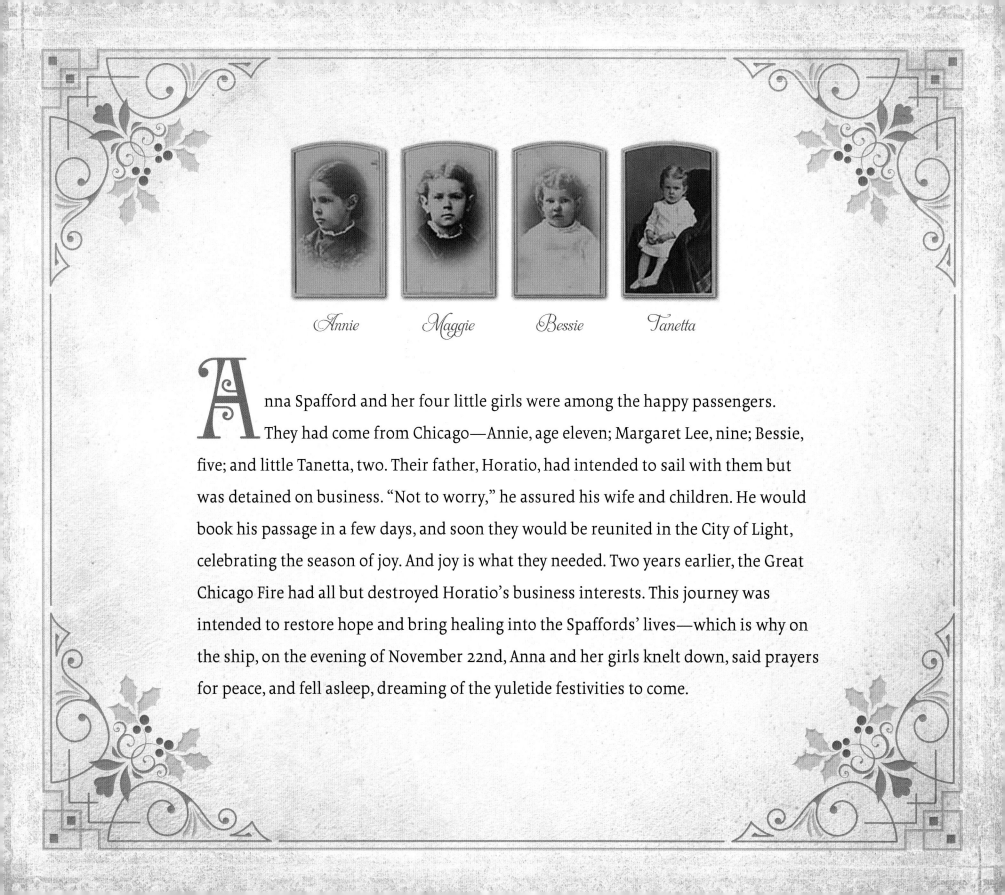

Annie   Maggie   Bessie   Tanetta

Anna Spafford and her four little girls were among the happy passengers. They had come from Chicago—Annie, age eleven; Margaret Lee, nine; Bessie, five; and little Tanetta, two. Their father, Horatio, had intended to sail with them but was detained on business. "Not to worry," he assured his wife and children. He would book his passage in a few days, and soon they would be reunited in the City of Light, celebrating the season of joy. And joy is what they needed. Two years earlier, the Great Chicago Fire had all but destroyed Horatio's business interests. This journey was intended to restore hope and bring healing into the Spaffords' lives—which is why on the ship, on the evening of November 22nd, Anna and her girls knelt down, said prayers for peace, and fell asleep, dreaming of the yuletide festivities to come.

At about two o'clock in the morning, they were jolted awake in their berths. Despite the night's clear, starry sky, the *Ville du Havre* had inexplicably collided with the *Loch Earn*, an iron-hulled Scottish clipper. Lifeboats quickly filled with people. Many passengers leapt into the icy waters. Anna tried desperately to keep her children together, but the two eldest became separated in the confusion. Just twelve minutes after the impact, a wave washed over the deck and Anna was drawn under the water with her youngest daughters.

Engraving depicting the last moments before the sinking of the Ville du Havre.

She held on to five-year-old Bessie until her strength gave out. Her last memory was of two-year-old Tanetta, in her delicate lace nightgown, torn from her grasp, getting smaller and smaller until she, too, finally disappeared. Later, the crew of the *Loch Earn* found Anna unconscious, floating on a wooden plank.

When the ship docked in Wales, Anna sent a telegram to her husband that began with the words, "Saved alone, what shall I do?"

Horatio immediately sailed from New York City. "There is just one thing in these days that has become magnificently clear," he wrote to a friend. "I must not lose faith."

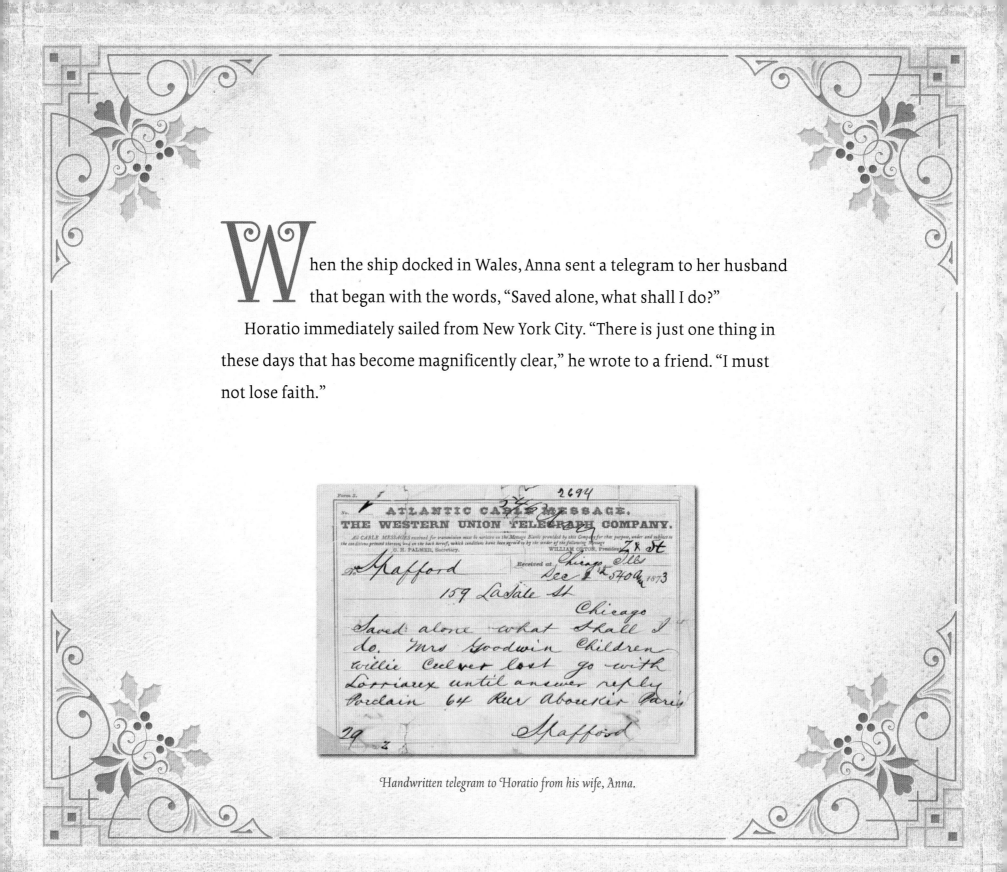

Handwritten telegram to Horatio from his wife, Anna.

Four days into his voyage, on a Thursday evening, the captain summoned Mr. Spafford to the foredeck. By the crew's calculations, they were nearing the place where Anna's ship had gone down, taking with it the bodies of their four daughters, now resting some three miles below. But Horatio refused to look down. "I did not think of our dear ones there," he later recounted. Instead, he gazed out across the rolling waves and up into the moonlit sky. There he began to formulate a simple expression of his faith—a verse that would become a beloved hymn.

> When peace like a river attendeth my way,
> When sorrows like sea billows roll,
> Whatever my lot, Thou hast taught me to say,
> It is well, it is well with my soul.

Only a few weeks earlier, in the same place on the open sea, Anna had experienced a similar awakening. After her rescue, when she regained consciousness, she was overcome with despair and wanted to throw herself back into the ocean. What was life worth now, and what could it ever be without her beloved children? But then, it was as if she heard a voice in her mind and her heart: "You are spared for a purpose, Anna. You have a work to do."

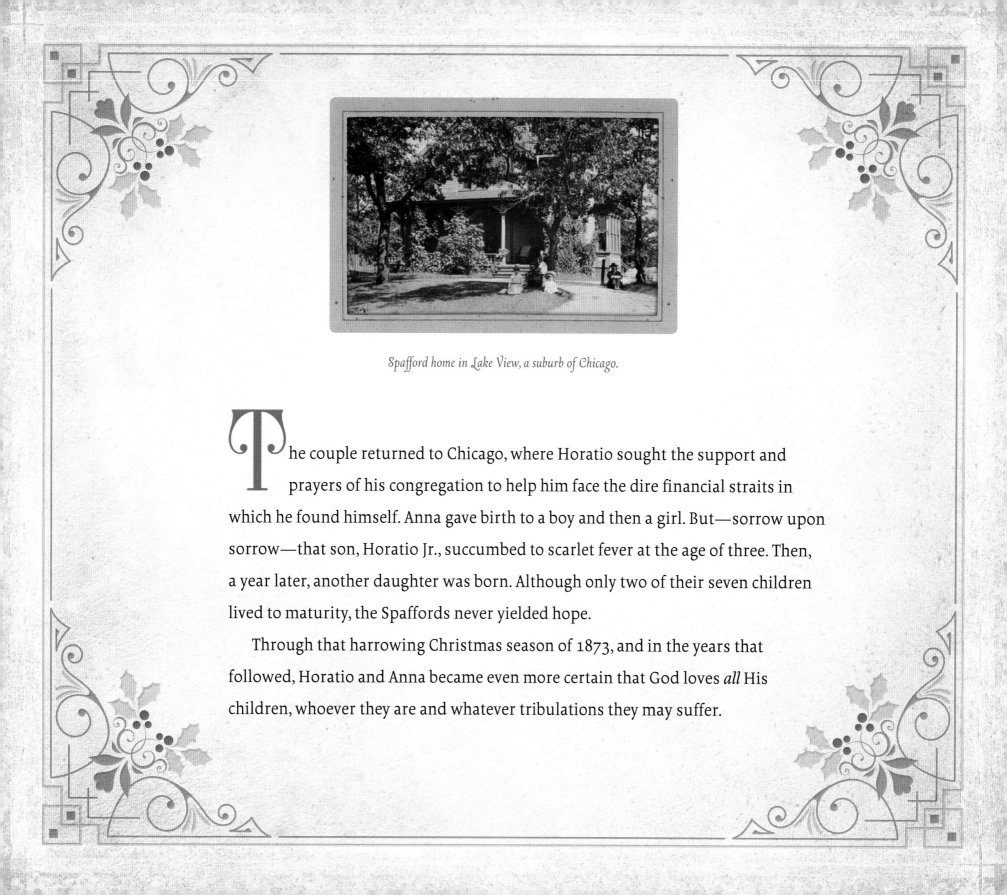

Spafford home in Lake View, a suburb of Chicago.

The couple returned to Chicago, where Horatio sought the support and prayers of his congregation to help him face the dire financial straits in which he found himself. Anna gave birth to a boy and then a girl. But—sorrow upon sorrow—that son, Horatio Jr., succumbed to scarlet fever at the age of three. Then, a year later, another daughter was born. Although only two of their seven children lived to maturity, the Spaffords never yielded hope.

Through that harrowing Christmas season of 1873, and in the years that followed, Horatio and Anna became even more certain that God loves *all* His children, whoever they are and whatever tribulations they may suffer.

In 1881, they moved their family to Jerusalem and established what they called the American Colony, not far from the "Little Town of Bethlehem" we celebrate at Christmas. Although they were deeply religious, their purpose was not to proselytize but to serve people of all backgrounds, relieving the effects of poverty, disease, and strife wherever they were found.

Seven years later, Horatio also died. Once again, Anna Spafford had reason to give up, but she did not. Every life has contradictions and imperfections, and hers was no exception. Yet, when it mattered most, in her most profound spiritual crisis, when all seemed lost, Anna found the strength to move forward and to turn outward—to continue what she and her husband had begun. And the seed of service they planted in others bore sweet fruit, indeed.

Members of the American Colony in Jerusalem, founded by the Spaffords.

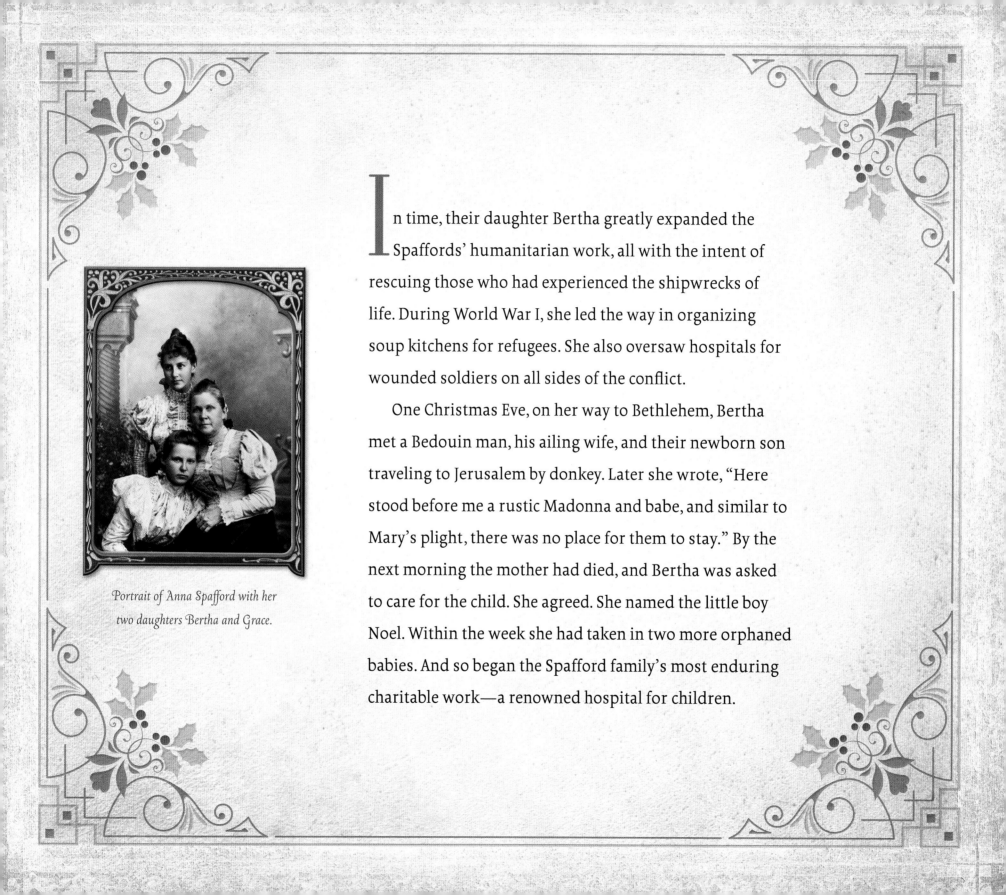

Portrait of Anna Spafford with her two daughters Bertha and Grace.

In time, their daughter Bertha greatly expanded the Spaffords' humanitarian work, all with the intent of rescuing those who had experienced the shipwrecks of life. During World War I, she led the way in organizing soup kitchens for refugees. She also oversaw hospitals for wounded soldiers on all sides of the conflict.

One Christmas Eve, on her way to Bethlehem, Bertha met a Bedouin man, his ailing wife, and their newborn son traveling to Jerusalem by donkey. Later she wrote, "Here stood before me a rustic Madonna and babe, and similar to Mary's plight, there was no place for them to stay." By the next morning the mother had died, and Bertha was asked to care for the child. She agreed. She named the little boy Noel. Within the week she had taken in two more orphaned babies. And so began the Spafford family's most enduring charitable work—a renowned hospital for children.

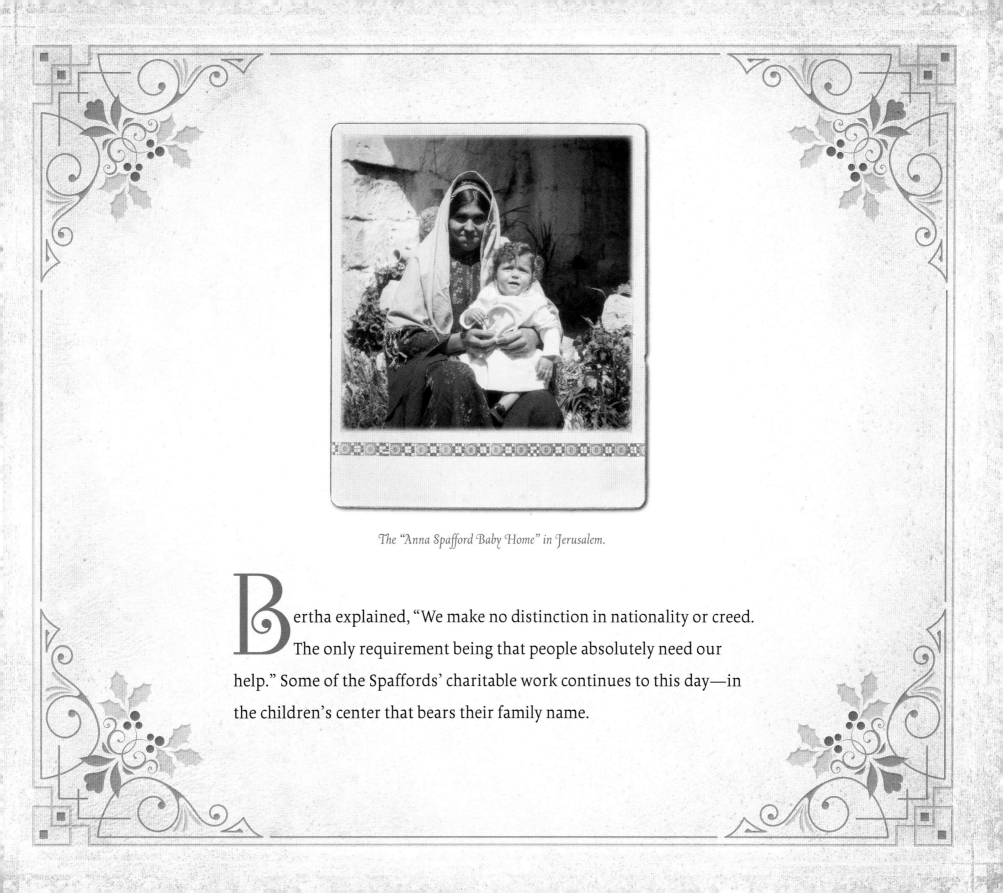

The "Anna Spafford Baby Home" in Jerusalem.

Bertha explained, "We make no distinction in nationality or creed. The only requirement being that people absolutely need our help." Some of the Spaffords' charitable work continues to this day—in the children's center that bears their family name.

For nearly 150 years, millions have sung and have been lifted by Horatio's hymn, "It Is Well with My Soul." Most have been unaware of the circumstances in which it was written, but they have been strengthened by its universal message. Horatio's words resound with the truth we celebrate at Christmas: a child *was* born in Bethlehem, bringing peace on earth and good will toward men. Because of Him, the human spirit can rise above tragedy. Whenever, however we suffer our own night of sorrow, His love does shine in the darkness. His peace can heal the wounded soul. And the Christmas work of giving, loving, serving, and rescuing is ours, if we choose to make it so. As we do, we join with saints and angels to rejoice and sing: "It is well, it is well with my soul!"

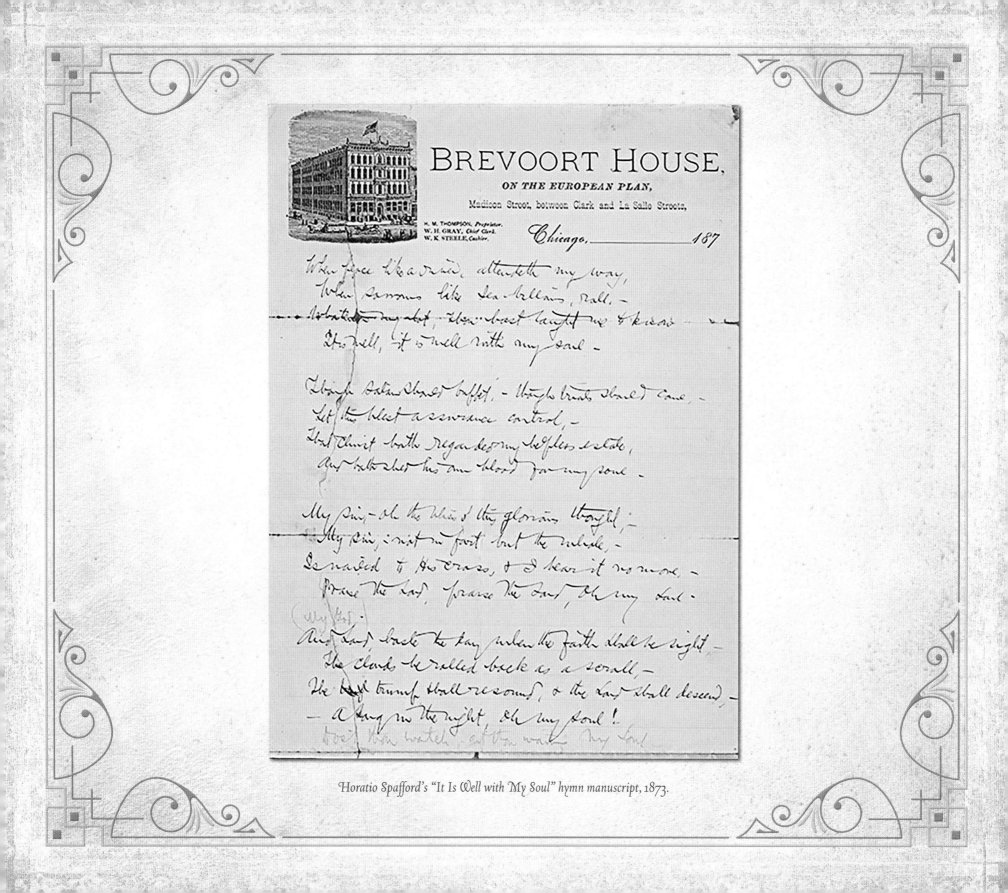

Horatio Spafford's "It Is Well with My Soul" hymn manuscript, 1873.

Lyrics from the hymn "It Is Well with My Soul"

By Horatio Gates Spafford

When peace like a river attendeth my way,
When sorrows like sea billows roll,
Whatever my lot, Thou hast taught me to say,
It is well, it is well with my soul.

Though Satan should buffet, though trials should come,
Let this blest assurance control,
That Christ hath regarded my helpless estate,
And hath shed His own blood for my soul.

My sin—oh, the bliss of this glorious thought!—
My sin, not in part but the whole,
Is nailed to the cross, and I bear it no more,
Praise the Lord, praise the Lord, O my soul!

For me, be it Christ, be it Christ hence to live:
If Jordan above me shall roll,
No pang shall be mine, for in death as in life,
Thou wilt whisper Thy peace to my soul.

But, Lord, 'tis for Thee, for Thy coming we wait;
The sky, not the grave, is our goal;
Oh, trump of the angel! Oh, voice of the Lord!
Blessed hope, blessed rest of my soul!

And, Lord, haste the day when the faith shall be sight,
The clouds be rolled back as a scroll;
The trump shall resound, and the Lord shall descend,
Even so, it is well with my soul.

Every December, one of the many wonders of Christmas in Salt Lake City is the annual concert of the Mormon Tabernacle Choir and Orchestra at Temple Square, a Temple Square tradition for decades. Since 2000, these popular concerts have delighted live audiences of over 60,000 people each year in the LDS Conference Center, with millions more tuning in to *Christmas with the Mormon Tabernacle Choir* on PBS through the partnership of WGBH and BYU Television. It is a full-scale production featuring world-class musicians, soloists, dancers, narrators, and music that delights and inspires viewers year after year.

Each concert has featured a special guest artist, including Broadway actors and singers Sutton Foster (2017), Laura Osnes (2015), Santino Fontana (2014), Alfie Boe (2012), and Brian Stokes Mitchell (2011); opera stars Rolando Villazón (2016), Deborah Voigt (2013), Nathan Gunn (2011), Renée Fleming (2005), Bryn Terfel (2003) and Frederica von Stade (2003); multiple Grammy Award–winner Natalie Cole (2009), *American Idol* finalist David Archuleta (2010); and the beloved Muppets® from Sesame Street® (2014). The remarkable talents of award-winning actors Hugh Bonneville (2017), Martin Jarvis (2015), John Rhys-Davies (2013), Jane Seymour (2011), Michael York (2010), and Edward Herrmann (2008) have graced the stage, sharing memorable stories of the season. The esteemed list of featured narrators also includes famed broadcast journalist Tom Brokaw (2012), two-time Pulitzer Prize–winning author David McCullough (2009), and noted TV news anchorman Walter Cronkite (2002).

The 360 members of the Mormon Tabernacle Choir represent men and women from many different backgrounds and professions and range in age from twenty-five to sixty. Their companion ensemble, the Orchestra at Temple Square, includes a roster of more than 200 musicians who accompany the Choir on broadcasts, recordings, and tours. All serve as unpaid volunteers, reflecting a rich tapestry of unique lives and experiences, brought together by their love of performing and their faith in God.

The Mormon Tabernacle Choir has appeared at thirteen world's fairs and expositions, performed at the inaugurations of seven US presidents, and sung for numerous worldwide telecasts and special events. Five of the Mormon Tabernacle Choir's recordings have achieved "gold record" and two have achieved "platinum record" status. Its recordings have reached the #1 position on Billboard® magazine's classical lists a remarkable twelve times since 2003.

This story of *It Is Well with My Soul* was originally written for the 2017 Christmas concert, narrated by Hugh Bonneville with music by the Choir and Orchestra. You can enjoy that performance at www.motab.org/itiswellwithmysoul.